Children's M

Children's Ministry has a commitment to provide the resources and training needed to help busy children's workers develop their ability to evangelise and disciple the children in their community.

Children's Ministry Guides are short, easy-to-read books offering practical insights into key areas of children's ministry. They complement the other resources and training opportunities available from Children's Ministry including:

- conferences
- training days
- distance learning course
- undated, activity-based, Bible-centred teaching programme
- books of ready-to-use ideas
- books of opinion and wisdom from children's ministry practitioners
- CDs and music books of children's praise songs
- supporting resources.

For more details about the Children's Ministry range of resources visit www.childrensministry.co.uk or call 01323 437748.

Other titles in the series

Dealing with Disruptive Children

ANDY BACK

with
Jenny Brown, Cathy Kyte,
Sue Price, Ruth Alliston

Series edited by Sue Price

CHILDREN'S
MINISTRY

EASTBOURNE

ISBN 1 84291 033 7

Published by
KINGSWAY COMMUNICATIONS LTD
Lottbridge Drove, Eastbourne, BN23 6NT, England.
Email: books@kingsway.co.uk

Book design and production for the publishers by
Bookprint Creative Services, P.O. Box 827, BN21 3YJ, England.
Printed in Great Britain.

Dedicated to
Nigel Waller
a man who exercises loving grace and gracious love
and to
Rachie Ross
a woman of perception, prayer, passion,
presence and proclamation

Contents

Acknowledgements

Without whom none of this would have been possible. . . I would count myself a privileged man to be part of either of these teams. But such is the blessing God is pouring out on me that I belong to them both.

Dunamis team

This is the youth work for 11–14s at Church of Christ the King, Brighton. I have served for many years under the leadership and oversight of Chris and Debbie Jarvis, who have provided much on-the-job training for me. With tears and laughter (mostly laughter) and many memoranda, we have discovered truths together and worked them out. We've experimented and learned. We've always tried to serve the young people as best we could, whatever personal sacrifices this demanded.

Now, working alongside the gifted leadership of Russ and Alex Lowman, I continue to learn. It's a joy to serve

God with you, and with the other members of the Dunamis team, past and present. It may be my name on the cover, but it's the lessons we have learned together that are on the inside.

Children's Ministry team

I have also been adopted into a wonderful, hilarious, gifted and interdependent team of writers, editors, consultants and exponents of ministry with kids of all ages. Under the expert editorial guidance and management of Sue Price, our various talents, churchmanship and specialisations have been blended into a coherent and significant force.

Thank you all for keeping me on the straight and narrow while allowing me to spray vast showers of sparks in all directions at once. The safety net of your kind but firm wisdom makes me strong, secure and, above all, happy to live on the edge.

Andy Back

Introduction

You've picked up this book for a reason. Perhaps you have discovered that there are children or young people in your care at church or in the classroom who have not responded first time to your polite requests. All you're asking them to do is to listen or to stop fidgeting, to sit down or to slow down, or (in extreme cases): 'Put down that axe, Eugene!'

This short, surface-skating guide to maintaining discipline, being self-disciplined, and knowing how to exercise corrective discipline may provide some insights from experience and some Bible wisdom. Our hope is that you can apply these principles to those lovable rogues, slippery scallywags and cheeky rascals (don't mention the thugs and hooligans) who populate and sometimes enliven your sessions on David and Goliath or Moses in the bulrushes.

Every child is unique (teenagers even more so) which means that there can be no hard and fast rules or easy answers. But it may be that as you check out this guide you'll light upon an idea that's worth trying with awkward Annie, boisterous Ben or complex Colin. As children develop, their needs vary, and their reactions to your expectations change, similarly. Nothing is very predictable, and the reasons for poor behaviour can be different at various ages, times of the year, physical surroundings, weather conditions, etc.

We shall explore the question 'Why?' and consider the various causes of disruptive behaviour: medical, chemical, social, spiritual, lack of training, sin and others. We shall attempt to define some terms and look at a superb, perfect example. And then the nitty-gritty. The guide will turn to 'How?' and offer various styles based on different value systems, with the advice and experience of successful discipline techniques and policies.

Each chapter concludes with issues to consider, which may help you to apply the principles. These can be used in personal study, or for discussion in your children's work team meetings or training times. Most of these points do not have a 'correct' answer, but they should provoke you to prayer, corrective action and a better understanding of how to deal with disruptive children.

Part One: Why?

1. We're all Sinners

I've been ministering to children and young people for almost two decades. Nice kids. From the quiet, sleepy streets of Hove, actually; daughter town to hustling, bustling Brighton before we were all lumped together as the City of Brighton and Hove.

Anyway, no inner-city problems here, thanks. Or so I thought when I started. No awkward youngsters to spoil our meetings, I reckoned. Except the trouble is, there has been a steady flow of disruptive young people through our doors. It seems, after all, that most families have their fair share of conflict, mistakes, selfishness, etc. Parents are not perfect, and they get it wrong sometimes. Children get it wrong. Young people also get it wrong, times without number. And the children's workers and youth leaders in our church have made many mistakes, too.

Why are some children disruptive? Why are they dismissive of authority, or even punishments? What is the source of the rebellious spirit? What is going on inside their heads? Are they just kicking up a fuss for the sake of it? Don't they know any better?

They are disruptive because they are sinners

> . . . for all have sinned and fall short of the glory of God.
> (Romans 3:23)

'Synne', after all, is an old-fashioned term borrowed by the writers of the Authorised Version of the Bible. When the archer's shot fails to reach the target, this is called a 'synne'. In the same way, when our feeble efforts at righteousness fall short of the standard God has set, we have committed 'sin'. It couldn't be more graphically illustrated!

We are all sinners (except those of us who have been gloriously saved from our sins by the death and resurrection of the Lord Jesus, who now declares us forgiven, righteous, blameless and saints). But you know what I mean. Everyone has rebelled and gone their own way; disruptive young people are sinners who are sinning.

CASE STUDY: FRANKLY ANGRY

Frank was a little lad who challenged authority at every opportunity. He knew how to look away just when you tried to gain eye contact. His dumb insolence was eloquent. His body language shouted, 'Keep Away!' to everyone – lots of aggression accompanied by a foul mouth.

He was fostered by the most loving and devoted of families, who showered him with wise love and firm guidelines. His reputation went before him, and as he progressed through the age groups, children's workers would tell grim tales in darkened prayer closets about Frank, his rebellion and wickedness. Even though we understood about the abuse to which he was subjected earlier in life, we could not stand back and allow his behaviour and attitude to dictate the tone of the meetings for the other children. It was appropriate to be sympathetic about the shabby treatment he had received at the hands of his biological parents, but it was not appropriate for us defeatedly to accept his anger and hostility. It was essential to love him, and for that love to be tough, helping to shape his behaviour and teach him the social skills he lacked.

We can be as understanding as it is possible to be about background, disadvantages or harsh treatment, but we must identify sin as sin and discourage it. Other chapters look at mitigating circumstances, such as poor role models in the home, lack of consistent application of rules or boundaries.

CASE STUDY: BILLY'S BORDERS

A church couple was going away for the weekend, and asked Pat and his wife to look after the kids. **Billy** *(8) was a ball of energy, and challenged the new authority several times on Saturday morning. So Pat sat him down and spelled out, over a bowl of ice-cream, the boundaries he was going to set, and said that if Billy stepped over the line, he would know about it. Post-neapolitan behaviour was respectful and calm, and remained within the boundaries for the rest of the weekend.*

Billy needed to know where Pat stood on several issues, and so a clear explanation of the rules and the penalties for infringements was all that was required to provoke excellent relationships – and that understanding resulted in a good time for all.

There is a lot of teaching in the New Testament about how the law demonstrates that we are sinners.

> The law was added so that the trespass might increase. (Romans 5:20)

> Sin, seizing the opportunity afforded by the commandment, produced in me every kind of covetous desire. (Romans 7:8)

But nevertheless, the existence of the Ten Commandments shows us the standards the Lord has set for us both in society and in our relationship with God. When children know precisely how far they can push us, or what limits we have set on rough play or cheeky comments, they are usually very adaptable and can work within those boundaries. Our part is to be realistic, consistent and loving.

They are disruptive because it's a spiritual battle

The Christian life isn't like a battle; it is one! The enemy of souls loves to discourage and batter us. When we start to feel that 'this kid is hopeless', the devil rejoices. When we say, 'I am hopeless,' he gets out the Vimto and Twiglets and has a party.

Why are we still surprised, when we intend to preach

the gospel and call for a response, that this is the meeting where the fire alarm is set off, the window in the boys' toilets gets broken and someone you trusted is caught red-handed pilfering from the tuck-shop? Or perhaps you've arranged for additional musicians to attend so that you can have a special time of worship, but they accidentally blow an electric fuse during their rehearsals and the buildings manager is on holiday. Or you've been fasting for a week to prepare yourself for issuing a challenge to the youth for radical commitment to Jesus, only to find that the people you had most in mind have all gone to a party and are not present to hear your God-given message.

There is an enemy at work here and he's both defeated and hurting. But in the meantime, he's prowling around like a roaring lion to see whom he can devour (1 Peter 5:8), and he's whispering temptation, discouragement and self-doubt into our ears 24/7.

How can we counter his attacks and imprisoning techniques? Here's a suggestion that I often fail to put into practice: make positive, biblical confession of truth. Turn with me, if you will, to Luke 4:1–13. Jesus famously dealt with the direct attacks of the enemy by declaring Scripture, and positively using godly truth to undermine the lies of the father of all lies. But I notice that this was the end of the story. Look again at verse 2.

. . . where for forty days he was tempted by the devil. He ate nothing during those days, and at the end of them was hungry. (Luke 4:2)

This is, arguably, one of the great understatements of the Bible. The devil tempted Jesus in an area of weakness; his physical need for bread was paramount, and so that's where the attack came. But we should not miss the fearsome reality that the devil tempted Christ for all of the forty days, not just with the final three direct suggestions recorded in the rest of this passage. The devil doesn't give up. A hungry lion returns again and again to attack the gazelles, until he gets his meat feast. He doesn't shrug his shoulders, shake his mane and call the pizza delivery shop.

The devil will go away and leave a Christian alone, provided we fulfil one of these criteria: resist (see James 4:7) or yield. The promise of the Scripture is great news. But most of us find relief from the pressure of temptation by giving in. 'The devil made me do it' is a poor excuse; he just suggested it and kept on and on at you until you caved in.

But the wonderful truth is that our enemy is also God's enemy, and that at the cross he was defeated. The shed blood of the Lord Jesus has destined the devil to the second death, the lake of unquenchable fire and destruction. But until the Lord's return in triumph, we still face a devil who is doing his best to undermine our faith and nullify our ministry with children and youth.

Little wonder, then, that if we are being strong, trusting God and walking in victory Satan will try another tactic; he'll get little Jessica to wind us up with her naughtiness and disrespect, or big Keith to provoke anger by his rudeness, disobedience and sneering attitude. Piece of cake, really.

It's a battle, friends, so let's not wander about without spiritual armour (see Ephesians 6:11–18).

TO CONSIDER

1. Why do you suppose Billy's behaviour was so much better once Pat had explained the rules and set the boundaries?
2. Take a few moments to think about the children or young people in your care who misbehave the most, and summon up grace and faith as you pray for them to stop sinning.
3. While we do not permit the excuse 'the devil made me do it', what degree of responsibility should be assigned to various bad behaviours?

2. Learned Behaviour

Parents, eh? I like this quote from a mature lady: 'If I'd known how much I was going to enjoy being a granny, I'd have skipped the stage of being a parent altogether!'

CASE STUDY: YOU'RE NOT MY LITTLE GIRL!

All three of his daughters (three years between each) have attended the children's work and the youth groups of the church. They are choice young women and have made significant contribution to the spiritual and social life of their contemporaries. I was invited for a meal in their home, and was surprised to see 14-year-old **Helen** *sit on her dad's lap and cuddle up. She's a bright, outgoing, sporty type. My surprise stemmed more from her willingness to show affection for her dad in front of me than from the act itself. I later quizzed her father about the incident.*

'I know she's 14. The little girl that used to cuddle up has grown into a woman. I understand that, and so does she, but sometimes, when she's at home, she's allowed to forget that she's

supposed to be a sophisticated young woman-about-town, and she can cuddle up to her old dad in safety and without question whenever she likes! I'd much rather Helen cuddled up to me than to some pimply youth who probably doesn't understand what love is, let alone what a father's love is!'

Far from that loving and secure home, where Dad has understood that his daughter is becoming a young woman, are many less happy families.

Strait-jacket

Bad behaviour from children and young people in church activities may stem from restrictive practices in the home. Too many rules or limiting factors can leave the young people ready to spread their wings and explore the perimeters of the rules of the club, which allows far more freedom than the home environment. The freedom is more than they can cope with, and, in their rejoicing exuberance, they may step over the line. It's not all their fault; they thought they could do more or less whatever they liked, compared to home life, and so they go wild.

When the wildness of their offspring is mentioned to the parents, they can hardly recognise the description of their children and tend to disbelieve or reassess their trust in the children's workers and youth leaders. The result is that, rather than supporting your polite suggestion that they teach restraint to their child, they may even resent your intervention to the point of complaining that your rules are too restrictive!

Run, run like the wind!

Another type of parent allows so much freedom and licence within the home that when the child arrives on Sunday morning, they expect to carry on with their giddy, carefree approach, despite its inappropriateness in a large setting. The child may take a while to process the news that the adults in charge in the church setting have different rules to the ones which apply at home. This is not a 'naughty child' situation; this is an 'ill-informed adult' issue!

Wrapped in cotton wool

I've also met parents who do not let their child out of their sight. No babysitters permitted; when the child was upset, he was put to the breast, up to age five (true); little friends visit him, but not vice versa, unless his mum goes too; home schooling, of course.

Church represents a challenge to this family, as there is little opportunity for the parents to pursue the long, tough, uphill road they have chosen for themselves. Does Mum regularly exclude herself from church meetings in order to accompany the child into the children's meetings? Is she welcome there? Does she have the skills that make her a welcome visitor? How do the other children cope? Or do the parents exclude their child from the children's meeting, forcing him to sit through the main event – week in, week out – eventually convincing him that church is dull?

It has to be said that there is little elbow-room within our church practices to allow for the macrobiotic parent, who has firm views on how they wish to bring up their child. Is it right that we expect every family to fit neatly into our little pigeon-holes? What about the smart child, or the slow learner? Are we putting them into the age group strictly according to age, or are we carefully taking into account the ability, friendship groups and siblings of each child? When does a guideline become a hard-and-fast rule?

CASE STUDY: LITTLE AND LARGE

Stuart was certainly undersized for his age, so when the time came for him to graduate from one youth group to the next, he requested that he stayed down, on account of his self-image. After considerable discussion, we agreed that he should be allowed to remain in the younger group, on the strict understanding that we would review this each term, based on his behaviour and the appropriateness of this arrangement being continued. As it worked out, he took this review process seriously, and became a valued and welcome member of the group, providing regular wit and stability to the younger kids, all of whom accepted him as one of their own.

By contrast, and even more successful, was the request by an understanding and youth-ministry-supportive parent that we consider allowing her daughter to graduate a year earlier. *Imogen* is an exceptionally gifted girl academically and spiritually, and had made excellent friendships with other girls, all of whom were about to move on to the other youth group. The unhappy accident of a September birthday was about to mean she'd be left behind. So we made an exception (slightly rubbery *rules are the best sort here); she is flourishing as a member of the older group, and our relaxed approach has borne fruit.*

Good behaviour doesn't just happen. The principle of original sin should help us to expect bad behaviour. Please note this doctrine of Total Depravity is nothing to do with being as wicked as possible, but speaks about being tainted with sin. It may not be the best analogy, but it's similar to pregnancy: you can't be partly pregnant or nearly pregnant; you either are or you aren't.

After all, you don't have to teach a little baby to be selfish, impatient or cranky. Rather, you have to train the little child to be obedient, to consider the concept of sharing or saying thank you, and stress that tantrums are unacceptable, and never result in the desired effect (unless you're in Tesco's).

So, good behaviour must be reinforced. It's only courtesy that when children and young people behave well, we should show our gratitude and respect to them for this. Sometimes, adults are ingrained with the thought that 'children ought to behave well, so rewarding good behaviour is a self-sustaining spiral of bribes'.

Ah, that may be so, but, in the first instance, while the children are getting to know your style, isn't there some lesson of respect and gratitude we can teach by rewarding good behaviour? I think there may be.

CASE STUDY: UNEXPECTED PRIZE

I was shocked and pleasantly surprised to be awarded the Most

Improved Team Player *award one year, when I was serving on an evangelism team. Of course, the first thing that went through my mind was: 'How terrible did I used to be?' but then I realised that the prize wasn't a criticism of the past, but a reward for the present. This encouraged me and spurred me on to love and good works (Hebrews 10:24).*

'Meet my needs' – demanding behaviour

Sometimes, children can respond very positively to the warmth or affection of the children's workers, and that is fine. But sometimes, the eagerness with which they receive the friendliness shows that they are not used to receiving this sort of care. While we will always be ready to comfort a child who is upset, and be willing to demonstrate warmth with appropriate physical touching, the wise children's worker will be careful and guard themselves from either showing or appearing to show favouritism. Indeed, the child who always wants to sit on the lap of a particular worker may be the love-sponge who will demand the attention of the worker to the detriment of the other children.

For the worker's safety, we recommend that sitting on laps is reserved for the upset young child, and is kept to a minimum. Don't reject a child by refusing attention, but deflect them by inviting them to sit on the chair or the floor next to you. A comforting arm around the shoulders for a moment may be appropriate. Having a standard like this does not deny the value of touch, or the need for children to recognise that the workers are approachable. But it protects the workers from the appearance of impropriety, from accusations of favouritism (or worse), and also from becoming so focused on one child that the others are neglected.

It is important to reserve physical contact for specific contexts. By all means, give a high five when a goal is scored at football or netball. Certainly, allow same-gender, side-on, arm-around-the-shoulder greetings. But when a teenage girl approaches a male worker with the intention of full-on hugging, my recommendation to the worker is to dodge and twist to prevent it. The girl is obviously comfortable with physical contact, but to encourage this by responding to it has an appearance that gives the wrong message to any observers. Other young people may feel this is a required ritual, or may not recognise that the teenager was initiating the contact. In today's society, we have to be seen to be squeaky clean, pure, blameless and diligent.

It's possible to deflect the hug without rejecting the child. The child may need the hug, true, but it's the parents' responsibility to provide hugs. Your children's meeting may very well be a safe environment. The child may very well feel safe in your meeting. But I'm afraid that's not a good enough reason to behave in a way that to some observers (who may not give you the benefit of the doubt) may have the appearance of impropriety. Your church can do without being associated with even a hint of a question on this matter.

The words *family* and *familiar* come from the same root. Let hugs and physical contact of this sort be encouraged in the family setting. It used not to be like this, but please face the fact that it is like this now. Sorry.

Where are they now?

Another key factor in the development of relationship between team members and children is the issue of the dreaded rota. In other words, when you're not here, you can't form a relationship with the youngsters. Only when you are present can this happen. OK, it's not rocket science, but I have come across children's work where each adult is on duty once every twelve weeks. This is entirely organised around the convenience of the adult, and is totally unhelpful to the child. One visit in three months means that every week the place is peopled by strangers. It is so unfair to expect to have authority, or to be obeyed, if the child isn't sure who you are or even if you're meant to be there.

Additionally, a rota like this sounds to me as if the adults would rather not be in the children's meeting at all. It would be much better to shed those adults who have a preference to be elsewhere, and then divide up the unfilled slots with people who would like to get to know the children or, much better, feel a calling to children's work.

Even then, my preference is for team members to work their duties consecutively, because then they will be present for more than one event at a time. For example, if the maths determine that a team member should be on duty for half of the events, it is far preferable for relationships' sake (and consequently discipline's sake, also) to work two

Sundays on, two Sundays off. Alternating just means that every week the child has to face someone new. If a team member works three on, three off, they are out of the main meeting for almost a month, which is not helpful, and they may find that they are running on fumes alone if they haven't been in a church meeting for that long. So our recommendation is to work two on, two off.

A few wise words from our sponsor

Now then, my sons, listen to me; do not turn aside from what I say . . . At the end of your life you will groan, when your flesh and body are spent. You will say, 'How I hated discipline! How my heart spurned correction! I would not obey my teachers or listen to my instructors. I have come to the brink of utter ruin in the midst of the whole assembly.' (Proverbs 5:7, 11–14)

This passage is part of a longer passage about avoiding prostitutes, which is far from our topic! But the deep regret for ignoring discipline being expressed struck me as a helpful warning.

TO CONSIDER

1. How can we help parents to make the transition from provider/carer to exasperating housemate as their offspring grow from children to young teens? Is there any hope for anything better than this?
2. Are there adjustments to the rota system you are using

that you could make to help better serve the children
and young people in your care?

3. Which children in your care expect personal attention?
   Are they favourites? Consider a strategy to help correct
   this imbalance without rejecting these children.

3. Medical Chemical Climatic

Not, as you may have wondered, an insurance company, but a selection of other influences on the behaviour of children.

Medical issues

Some children are ill, or have a poor diet, due to incompetence or poverty at home. Fish finger and ketchup sandwiches followed by a bowl of Coco Pops may sound like a treat, but when it's the pinnacle of culinary creativity, the alarm bells should be ringing. Sadly, a lot of mothers are achieving little more than this, and their children do not receive their RDA of vitamins, minerals, protein or carbohydrates.

The poor or incomplete diet can have a significant impact on the child's ability to sit and learn. Similarly, the child whose e-numberstream is tainted with real blood will be hard to predict, except that we can be sure the behaviour will be unacceptable. Food additives have been shown to affect the responses children have to various stimuli. Hand out fruit-flavoured little timebomb sweeties just before you start your sessions and you might as well not bother to try to gain attention. For older kids, rapid consumption of cans of fizzy sugar drinks has a similarly scary effect.

Have you ever considered that little Kevin's disruptive behaviour may stem from the undiscovered fact that he cannot see or hear too well? He needs to be encouraged (requested, commanded) to sit near the front, so that he can see what's going on and hear everything that you say. If he can't see, or can't hear, he'll get bored, and when he gets bored, your sessions get more interesting than you were anticipating.

Chemical

Poor attention or disruptive behaviour may even be the result of inhaling or smoking chemicals, too. Glue-sniffing (solvent abuse) gives a quick, cheap and very effective fix, and sends the user so high that they don't care whether or not they are in trouble with those attempting to supervise them. These kinds of product are very easy to obtain.

You probably don't have children or young people in your group at church or school who are using drugs, do you? Or do you? How could you tell? Poor or disruptive behaviour is one sign among many. Check for glazed eyes, rashes around the nose and mouth, and deteriorating complexion, teeth, attention and memory.

A recent report even suggested that some children turn

up at school hung over. Others fail to attend for the same reason. It couldn't happen here, could it? Symptoms to watch for include negative reactions to noise and light, feeling groggy, and responding positively to offers of 'hair of the dog'!

Attention deficit

ADD (Attention Deficit Disorder) and ADHD (Attention Deficit and Hyperactivity Disorder) are now medical diagnoses which, while not excusing bad behaviour, help to explain it in terms of a mental illness or affliction. There is a thin line between this and excusing bad behaviour as a symptom of an affliction, but it's a line we have to walk.

CASE STUDY: CAN'T READ, WON'T READ

Darren was one of those 'troublesome' boys about whom we were told a great deal by colleagues who were volunteers for young age groups. He left a trail of horror stories about violence, insolence, disregard for authority, disrespect and several other minor crimes. When I met him, he tried it on (testing to see how far he could push). I think I handled him with firm grace. His career through the youth group was tempestuous and patchy, punctuated by temporary bans. However, when he was twelve the education system sent him for tests, and he was diagnosed as being dyslexic. This, apparently, explained all his bad behaviour; he couldn't read properly and was being held back by this; he was frustrated in lessons and therefore behaved badly.

Now, I'm absolutely convinced that dyslexia is a crippling and hard-to-diagnose affliction that can have a serious effect on a student's ability to keep up with the rest. A friend of mine is seriously dyslexic, but his word processor's spell checker saved him a lot of trouble and got him through his Oxford degree in Theology and into the Baptist ministry. When I think about it, it was actually his determination to succeed, despite his reading/writing difficulties, which made the greater contribution.

Darren, however, plays on his dyslexic diagnosis, has completely lost interest in obedience, rules, authority and being acknowledged. This could possibly be part of the symptoms.

However, he could just be a naughty boy who loves to sin, who prefers the attention of punishments to being ignored when he's good, and has learned how to fool some wishy-washy child psychiatrist/sociologist/behavioural fudge-merchant somewhere who wants to excuse or deny human sin.

Or perhaps Darren has got to me. Who can tell?

Of course, ADD and ADHD are serious illnesses which we must take seriously. The difficulty comes when we are faced with a group of children, one of whom is a sufferer. Our sensitivity to the sickness and to protecting the sufferer may lead us into what looks like injustice.

Why are we seen apparently to accept the bad behaviour of one when we actively discourage or punish similar offences committed by another child? How can we explain this, without resorting to such phrases as 'He can't help it', or 'She's not herself today'? God has placed within all the other children a mechanism known as 'natural justice', and they will quickly develop Solomon-sized ability to judge what is fair and what isn't.

Rain, rain, go away

In conversation with school teachers, I discovered that one of the key factors in the expectation they have of each lesson is weather conditions.

CASE STUDY: BOUNCING OFF THE WALLS

Alastair, a secondary school geography and sociology teacher, testifies: 'The state of the weather has a huge impact on discipline. If it's sunny and warm, the mood is generally good, but some want to be outside. Dull or average weather is boring but acceptable, so it doesn't make much difference. Rain is the worst, because the kids can't go outside at lunchtime, and by the afternoon they're bouncing off the walls with energy and have no way of dissipating it except by disrupting my class. Fights break out, along with running in corridors, shouting and total lack of concentration. The last thing they want to do is sit quietly.

'Snow is good, because they can have fun with that, and I can always use wintery conditions to talk about glaciers, pack ice, freeze-thaw effects, soil erosion, fjords, and...' (transcript ends, due to interviewer dropping off to sleep, induced by boredom).

Some children misbehave because church meetings feel like school – too much emphasis on learning and not enough on fun. Or perhaps the child is unsettled at school and brings this lack of contentment to the Sunday event as well.

TO CONSIDER

1. Identify any children in your care who suffer (or may suffer) from poor diet, optical or auditory challenges, substance abuse or ADD. What adjustments to the way you interact with these children can you make to help them further?

2. What difference does weather make to the way you feel? How can you make adjustments to your children's meetings to take these effects into account?

4. Dysfunction

This unattractive, hybrid word describes families where the normal workings have been disrupted in some way. The breakdown of marital relationships has a devastating effect on children, and this is often seen in changed behaviour, attention seeking, rage, self-hatred and so on. Children may believe (mistakenly) that they are the reason why Daddy left, or why the rows became so bitter and vindictive. They may be uprooted and taken to live with grandparents or other relatives, while new accommodation is sought. They may have to deal with getting to know Dad's new girlfriend or Mum's new boyfriend, and then there is the issue of meeting and learning to live with Dad's new girlfriend's other children.

Dysfunction is not just about marriage breakdown. It includes families where one parent has died, or where a child has died. It also affects the children of unmarried mums, who are trying to be both mother and father. This can also be complicated by a succession of short-term 'uncles' who visit and stay, and then go again. Understandably, children in this environment quickly lose the will to trust men, or to expect consistency from adults.

It is important to stay informed of changes that take place at home, as this will certainly have implications for the way the children behave and their openness to correction or direction.

How wise and loving God is, to provide the protective, consistent and functional institution of marriage, with sanctity before and during, providing children with security and worth!

Victims twice over

Required reading for all children's and youth workers is the shattering *A Child Called It* by Dave Pelzer. His story, a combination of systematic neglect and violent abuse at the hands of a disturbed mother, is appalling, especially since it is written with a young boy's viewpoint and vocabulary. His misunderstanding of The Mother's demands is clear, as well as his desire to please her and win her love. Eventually, he recognises that obedience will only ever spare him from the worst of the cruel and unusual punishments she devises for him. Her attempts at murder become increasingly close to success, and the reader at times can understand the child's wish for her to achieve her goal, and put him out of his miserable life.

His starvation leads him to a life of crime, stealing food at school and becoming disruptive and difficult to control. His exhausted rages gain only disciplinary measures, and his bruised and damaged body is interpreted by teachers as evidence that he is getting involved in fights, too. The despair is finally relieved when a part-time teacher recognises that his bruises and emaciated state are the result of sustained, brutal abuse.

While Pelzer's story is extreme, it alerted me to the danger of misinterpreting disruptive behaviour. In his case, it was a cry for help against someone he wanted to love, not accuse. His thefts were motivated by need, not sin, attention-seeking, or bad weather. But he was a victim twice over, abused by his mother and ignored or punished by the school system that failed to observe his plight (albeit a well-kept secret).

I know of a number of abused children and young people who have come through our church children's work. What frightens me is this: how many others were abuse victims we never recognised? What more can we do to show the love and mercy of God to these children?

It's vital that every church has a Child Protection Policy, and that every worker is not just police-checked but also trained in responding to children who disclose abuse. It must not be a case of clumsy, ill-informed guesswork. And it must never be that we assume wrong-doing on the part of parents. Some kids bruise easily, and others do fall down the stairs – but not every week. Let's be diligent, loving, faithful, merciful and responsible.

For more information (including suggestions for establishing a Child Protection Policy in your church) contact: Churches' Child Protection Advisory Service, PO Box 133, Swanley, Kent BR8 7UQ. Helpline: 01322 660011.

TO CONSIDER

1. Is it possible that there are abused (neglected, beaten or sexually abused) children in your children's meetings? How can you identify them?

2. How adequate is your church's policy for helping abused children who make disclosures to you or other children's workers in your team? Are all your workers sufficiently trained? What if the pastor's child makes an accusation against him?

5. Natural Teenage Rebellion

The mostly entertaining exploits of comedian Harry Enfield's character 'Kevin the teenager' provide insights into the sinister cloud which descends over lovely twelve-year-olds as midnight strikes on their thirteenth birthday. The speaking voice becomes a grunt or a shout; expressions of affection boil down to 'I hate you!'; communication between parents and offspring crashes and burns; the young person is at the centre of a world which contains nothing else of any value.

We smile and sometimes dare to describe the humour as 'well-observed', but when the reality bites, it's not so funny.

Teenagers are a relatively recent phenomenon. The term was coined as recently as the 1950s; before the Second World War, children became adults at 21. Many of them would have been joyfully following Father down the pit, into the factory, or onto the 6.53 to London Bridge for several years. But with the baby boomers came leather jackets, motorbikes, James Dean, the curled lip and a shift in attitude. Suddenly, young people stood out as a significant section of society; they had money without much responsibility (no gas bills, mortgages, or nappies to buy); they had time on their hands and rebellion in their souls.

Obviously, that's too sweeping an analysis, but the general trend from the 1950s has been that there is an increasingly large sector of society with money to burn and the means to start a fire. We ignore this trend at our peril.

So, armed with that little bit of social history, then, teenage rebellion . . .

Defiance

The key question is: 'Who's in charge?' Within the minds of rebels, the answer 'The adult' appears to be incorrect. It's a constant battle, and it's fought in the corridors of schools, in the living rooms of homes and in the classrooms of church buildings as well.

CASE STUDY: TONY, LESS THAN THE BEST

Perhaps the most frustrating attempts at connecting with a young person have involved **Tony** *(eleven, going on eight), a lonely young man who avoids eye contact, smiles to himself as he ignores rules, and refuses to be reasoned with when challenged. He seems unable to make friends (or is at least untrained and inexperienced in this essential skill), and ends up seeking attention, which results in further rejection or, much worse, bullying. He seems to accept harsh words, criticism, mockery and finally* rejection as life's lot, since that's all he has ever known.

While we work hard to eliminate bullying, Tony seems to have the victim self-image. There is a timebomb of pent-up anger at all this rejection and lack of expression, and sadly his mother's attitude is to smother him and treat him like the seven-year-old she would probably prefer him to have stayed.

It's hard to understand why he wants to stay at the youth club when it's time for him to leave (older teens remain for an exclusive hour), when he appears to have been having such a horrible time all night so far. But he runs away and hides, or escapes our disciplinary clutches, runs through the fire escape and bunks over the wall. His latest 'crime' was to pinch a baseball cap from little Kevin and throw it into a neighbouring garden over a wall. Kevin's father is not on our team, and thus is not limited by the Children Act, so he grabbed Tony, restrained him and began to shout at him, asking what right he thought he had to behave thus with other people's property.

The smile with which Tony greets attention was in evidence as he wriggled, slipped free, ran for it and occupied three team members in looking for him in the local street for the next 20 minutes – not Kevin's dad, you understand, who shrugged his shoulders, climbed over the wall to retrieve his son's cap, and then drove away. Thanks, mate!

By the time we decided to call his home to inform his parents that Tony had made himself scarce, he was safe and well and eating toast in front of the TV. Apparently, the father had arrived by car to collect his wayward son as Tony flew around a corner; the boy climbed aboard, and they drove away, all out of sight of any of the youth team. Frustrating!

When we try to speak to Tony about his attention-seeking/

victim behaviour, he looks away, smiles, refuses to acknowledge and seems to accept exclusion as just another rejection. It pains us to add to his burden, but to allow his behaviour to go unchecked paints a message in 4-foot (1.3 metre) high letters to the other members of the youth club.

Hormone-induced confusion

Young people are just realising that the difference between the genders means more than just preferences about floral bedspreads or an inability to catch a ball. At exactly the same time as appearance takes on paramount importance in the process of attracting others, the spectre of acne strikes, rendering otherwise porcelain-like complexions into pepperoni pizza. Their bodies are preparing themselves for adulthood several years before there is the slightest chance of social, moral or spiritual boundaries being extended to include permission for the unleashing of the various enthusiasms with which their bodies are crammed. In the meantime, of course, they must still obey their parents, keep their rooms tidy, say please and thank you, do their homework and tolerate their annoying little brothers.

It's no surprise, therefore, that hitherto nice children become a raging ferment of pent-up aggression, confusion, frustration and worry.

Look at me!

It should also be little surprise that attention seeking, while a serious problem in children, becomes a major issue when puberty strikes. It's a competitive world out there, and young men are battling (sometimes physically fighting) each other to win the attention of the girls. Trouble is, the girls have realised that the boys are, by and large, still mere boys, and that the young men a couple of years older are far more appealing.

Adults are fools; the media tell me so

There is a dangerous trend in entertainment for children and young teens which constantly underlines the suggestion that children are superior and adults are at best foolish.

Bart Simpson's attitude to adults is distorted by the lousy role models with which he's surrounded: his fully dysfunctional father, Homer; the 'Christian' lunatic, Ned Flanders; the slobs in the bar; Mr Burns; the criminal clown, and so many more. Aladdin's experience of adults was that they were weak kings, scheming evildoers or thieves. Soap parents have their own problems, and are thus too self-obsessed to deal effectively with their kids. The Jackson parents have abandoned their single-parent daughter and mindless son; *Neighbours* kids are either running wild or are over-protected; Grange Hill School is a zoo, but the keepers haven't been told they are in charge. OK, that's slightly strong, but you take the point.

Testing, testing

Throughout a child's development to adulthood, the rules

are relaxing, the perimeters of permission are expanding, and the command centre of their lives is become increasingly internalised. So, a lot of experimentation is required to discover exactly what today's changes allow or disallow.

During puberty, this is at the max, and when the natural, innocent testing of ever-changing rules is mixed with the rebellious, sinful confusion of hormone-induced change, there are going to be sparks!

TO CONSIDER

1. In what ways did you rebel as a teenager? What actions or attitudes helped you back onto the straight and narrow (assuming you've managed to return to the straight and narrow, that is!)?
2. How undesirable is conflict?

6. Poor Teaching Style

You know, self-doubt aside, we really ought to allow for the possibility that we are poor teachers, or dull communicators, or boring people, or lacking in skill or training.

Not us, obviously (neither you nor me). But if not us, then maybe others. The mistakes they make can err on the side of over-preparation or lack of it. Perhaps they exercise heavy-handed crowd control, or ineffective attempts to ask for attention; or maybe they are afflicted with an unhelpful voice (squeaky, thin, metallic). It might be their selection of attire (dangerously unfashionable or ludicrously trendy mutton dressed up as lamb). Are they relying on chalk and talk (or even just talk) or content-light, style-heavy sound-bites of video clips, drama, interviews, songs, ice-breaker games etc? Look carefully at the spaces between the lines, dear reader, and you may meet me and my manifold mistakes; some are behind me, some probably still lurk in ambush.

But we are foolish to assume that 100 per cent of the

responsibility for disruptiveness or bad behaviour must be laid at the feet of the children or young people. Captivate their interest, or emotions, or imagination, or thinking, and the session may not run smoothly or predictably, but it has a much better chance of staying on topic. Put succinctly: bored kids muck about.

I have been in many a children's and young people's meeting (as an adult, and as a child myself) where the speaker stood silently, waiting for the hubbub to cease and the excited youngsters to give their attention to the front. I cannot help myself thinking that this is a technique which may have worked in the past, but which is really an arrogant expectation that the authority of the speaker is sufficient to subdue.

Ask yourself, do the children go quiet in hushed reverence and respect when you enter the room? I hope not! I hope some rush to you to tell you about an adventure or scrape they've got into, or to be the first to tell you last time's memory verse, or to introduce their friend, who is attending for the first time, or (best of all) to offer you chocolate.

Please don't stand at the front and wait for quiet. It may never happen! Instead, be fascinating. Do conjuring tricks. Tell a funny story. Draw pictures on the overhead projector. Play a video. Remove your jumper (careful now!). In other words, make it worth their while to stop their conversation. Provide something better for them to do.

My teaching style depends on this technique, but I have also learned that grabbing attention isn't the same as keeping attention. You can't spend the whole time doing exciting things like eating daffodils, demonstrating your skills at keepy-uppy or drinking a yard of Irn-Bru. Rather, you have to maintain attention in easy stages by making sure you are worth listening to throughout the message. The harsh reality is that it takes a fresh effort of the will every 3.5 seconds to keep concentration! So in your ten-minute presentation, are you rewarding the 170 efforts that the children or young people are making? I am not suggesting that you need to grab attention 170 times (phew!), but the truth is that if you set yourself the target of rewarding at least half of the efforts of will, you need to be worth attention 85 times.

How can you be that interesting? Consider using the action clip of the video, rather than the talking heads clip. Provide lots of visuals to go with the CD track you want to play. Dramatise the Bible story. Ask three young people to read the scripture aloud (either three sections of the passage or a short passage three times) and award prizes for the best reading, according to an audience clapometer. Teach the memory verse through the talk, not just at the end. Ask questions, and invite interactivity. Don't just wave your arms about; have a meaning for each gesture, and make it count. Avoid getting trapped behind a table or (worse) a lectern. Walk about. Maintain eye contact with individuals for a lot longer than you do at the moment. Don't scan the audience or speak to the back wall. Look at people. Smile a lot more than you do at the moment. Laugh, if possible.

Sounds impossible? Probably. But how dare we take the message of life and present it in a dull way! What foolishness to treat the gospel in a way that communicates that we agree with our audience that it is tedious and unimportant!

Enough! Sorry to rant, but without grasping this point, we speak and speak and no one listens and the word of God is trampled underfoot and treated the same way that you treated those bad lessons you had at school where the clock dragged and the bell refused to ring.

God's word is 'living and active and sharper than any two-edged sword', so let's keep our Bible talks lively, active, short and sharp.

TO CONSIDER

1. Try to recall the main points of the teaching given at last week's children's meeting. Draw conclusions according to your accuracy/success in this consideration.

2. Try to apportion the percentage of responsibility for poor behaviour you should accept from your last children's event. Don't be too hard on yourself, but how could you have improved your teaching style to engage the particular children who caused the greatest disruption?

Part Two: How?

Part Two: How

7. Discipline Is a Practical Issue

We all know what we mean by the word *discipline*, so it's unlikely that we all mean the same thing. Thus, it's a good idea to pause at this stage and examine what meanings the word contains, and unpack a few.

Learning

A student reading, say, English at university can say that his discipline is humanities; a physics student's discipline is, obviously, physics; an engineering student's discipline is non-existent. But the word can mean learning.

In the case of the children or young people in our sessions, our goal is to provide didactic input as well as to demonstrate love, purpose, to set a good example of godliness, and to give opportunities for prayer, corporate worship, spiritual gifts, etc.

Obedience to instruction

When everything works as it should, the student not only has a learning experience, but also applies the teaching with obedience to God.

Drill

In the past, many uniformed church youth organisations taught children and young people to march up and down the hall – by the left, quick march, left turn, mark time, stand at . . . Ease!

The skills required to stay in time and in formation are discipline in a practical form. My dad taught the boys in his Pathfinder unit to drill so well that they had a seven-minute display of drill, which they performed without any commands being issued – the boys would count the steps and remember the moves. Amazing! A bygone era (1950s), of which we will never see the like again!

Maintaining order

Please note that discipline is about maintaining order – present continuous tense, I believe. Not just attention grabbing, but so much more than that. It requires appropriate and interesting teaching, and involved concentration from the children.

Mental and moral trained condition

The battle for the mind is a gigantic struggle; as soon as we have tamed one thought, we need to take another captive; little wonder the Bible is full of instructions on the topic. We must set our minds on Christ, on meditation of the word; we do well to dwell on the word, to exercise ourselves in Scripture memory and to being transformed by the renewing of our minds as well.

When our minds are trained, renewed, set on Christ, and filled with God's word, we stand a slight chance of being able to take captive evil thoughts and thus resist temptation.

A system of rules

Probably the least helpful of the definitions. The law shows us the will of God, but his grace motivates us to walk in his ways. We will never please God by our obedience to rules, since he's already thrilled to bits with us. But people who are disciplined are those who live as God intends and love him with a whole heart.

Control over church members

There was once a time when some churches were criticised for 'heavy shepherding'. This expression was used to indicate demands made by church leaders over what were assumed to be simple, mindless, sheep-like church members.

These may have been legitimate criticisms or accusations based on misunderstandings. Whatever the truth of the matter, there is a positive aspect to the authority God has given to those charged with leading the flock of God. They offer more than just random opinions; the expectation on church leaders is that they have godly wisdom, at least.

> The elders who direct the affairs of the church well are worthy of double honour, especially those whose work is preaching and teaching. (1 Timothy 5:17)

So don't just show respect; double their wages!

Chastisement

Ah, now then. This meaning of the word is about punishment and beatings. The world has taken this meaning and muddled it with perverse behaviour and sado-masochism, rubberware and so on.

But when the headmaster tells the scallywag schoolboy: 'This will hurt me more than it hurts you', this is discipline providing corrective shaping of the will of the child, as well as issuing pain in exchange for minor crimes. Obviously, these days corporal (bodily) punishment is frowned upon, but the Bible still tells us that the man who spares the rod hates his son (Proverbs 13:24). The loving shepherd in Psalm 23 also had a rod which was primarily a device for counting the sheep, so he'll know if there are only 99, but also could be used to encourage the sheep into the right direction.

Remember, these were days long before Phil Drabble and that long whistle: 'Come by, come by.'

CASE STUDY: SERIOUS OFFENCE, SERIOUS PUNISHMENT

Charlene had been cheeky to her mother, and she was sent to her room. Dad soon arrived home and had a conversation with his wife and then came upstairs to have a chat with his nine-year-old daughter.

'You were rude to Mum, weren't you?'

'Yes, I was.'

'You know what this means, don't you?'

She knew it meant the wooden spoon, but she didn't say.

'Someone's got to die,' said Dad.

'Die?' asked Charlene, not quite believing that mild-mannered old Dad was saying this. She quickly glanced out of the window to see if he'd built a gallows in the back garden. Fortunately not. But what could he mean?

Dad went on to explain. When we sin, we need forgiveness. Forgiveness comes by the shedding of blood. Jesus had to die in order for Charlene to be forgiven for breaking the fifth commandment: honour your father and mother. He felt she was old enough to be taught that sin has important consequences.

Dad and Charlene prayed together, asking God to forgive her sin, and then the wooden spoon came out as a reminder. Tears, cuddles, giggles followed. Then Charlene spoke to her mother and received forgiveness.

But she learned that when she sins, someone has to die for that sin to be forgiven.

Political correctness and a great deal of wisdom have thankfully outlawed physical beatings from teachers (and children's workers). But there is an appropriate role for chastisement within the home, it would seem.

However, chastisement of a non-physical sort is still an option. Withdrawal of privileges, insisting that the guilty one sits at the front of the room, deselecting them from the list of people going on the outing – all of these are legitimate.

TO CONSIDER

1. Identify three occasions when disciplinary correction might have been more effective in shaping a child's behaviour than the less confrontational approach that you chose to use.

2. Over which issues is it acceptable for a member of a church to refuse to submit to those in spiritual authority over him?

3. If Charlene's dad went too far in his attempt to teach her the seriousness of sin, how would you advise him to moderate his lesson?

8. Self-discipline

This is a vitally important skill that we all need to learn. It takes self-discipline to remain an ex-smoker, to stick to a diet, to make all the arrangements necessary to achieve happiness on your wedding day, and to write a book. It takes self-discipline to train your body to the peak of physical fitness (I expect), and it takes self-discipline to remain calm when the children in your session decide to play up.

> For God did not give us a spirit of timidity, but a spirit of power, of love and of self-discipline. (2 Timothy 1:7)

It is a central part of the activity of the Holy Spirit to help us exercise self-control (also translated self-discipline). It's a fruit of the Holy Spirit (Galatians 5:22–23), and it's integral to the spiritual growth described in 2 Peter 1:5–7. We add self-discipline to knowledge, and add perseverance to self-discipline. David spends half the Psalms speaking to his soul, and taking control. Praise the Lord, O my soul!

> For you, O God, tested us; you refined us like silver. You
> brought us into prison and laid burdens on our backs. You let
> men ride over our heads; we went through fire and water, but
> you brought us to a place of abundance. (Psalm 66:10–12)

This testing has produced the best possible result. Not failure or resentment, but abundance and gratitude. Few of us have iron will, but God has given us a spirit of self-discipline, so let's not deny it by habitually sinning or by a haphazard lifestyle.

And let's not forget that setting a consistently good example to the children and young people will have a positive effect upon them. It may not be immediate, but it will happen!

Perfect self-discipline

Without doubt, Jesus is the best example of a perfectly self-disciplined man. From the incident in the Temple, when he was an adolescent, to the calmly focused pastoral moments with Peter on the beach, his life was characterised by self-control. Of course, he also exhibited many other fruits and gifts of the Holy Spirit, and they were always perfectly subjected to the will of God.

> When Joseph and Mary had done everything required by the
> Law of the Lord, they returned to Galilee to their own town of
> Nazareth. And the child grew and became strong; he was
> filled with wisdom, and the grace of God was upon him.
> (Luke 2:39–40)

How many children aged between 0 and 12 (for this is the period covered here) do you know who can be genuinely describe as strong, wise and gracious? Jesus was without sin, and this of course includes his childhood. He learned at his father's workshop as any tradesman's son might have done, but he never set fire to the cat in a moment's irresponsible speculative experimentation. He played with other children, but was never spiteful or selfish or rude; his school teachers must have been very impressed with his wisdom, and stunned by his exemplary behaviour. He was never late with his homework assignments; never held back for a detention; never caught scrumping, salting snails or smoking behind the bike sheds. He never downloaded copyright-protected MP3 files through the school PC direct to his mini-disc when he should have been learning the periodic table of elements or the names of the minor prophets in chronological order.

But this perfect, holy child isn't just a virtuous nothing that never has fun, never enjoys the company of naughty children, never runs and laughs through the streets of the town. He was superbly normal, without being tainted by the sinful nature of the others. It's hard to imagine such a child, but when we look at the way he dealt with conflict and temptation through his ministry and as he prayed in Gethsemane, we acknowledge that he was without sin.

His parents took him to the Temple every year, but when he was twelve, he became so involved in discussions with the teachers that he didn't leave when Mary and Joseph did. This wasn't wilful defiance, youthful irresponsibility, or even careless timing. The mistake was made by Mary

and Joseph in assuming Jesus was in the crowd somewhere, running with his pals and having a good time out
of the clutches of parents. It seems as if their expectation
was that he would be with other youngsters, having fun
without getting into trouble. But when they discovered he
wasn't there, they returned to Jerusalem.

> 'Why were you searching for me?' he asked. 'Didn't you know
> I had to be in my Father's house?' (AV '. . . wist ye not that I
> must be about my Father's business?') (Luke 2:49)

His words are not reproachful or disrespectful to his parents; simply a reminder that he was set apart. He was
Immanuel; he was a gift sent to save mankind from its sins.
Thus, they should adjust their expectations of him. They
should wist that he was going to be about the business of
his heavenly Father. They should have wisted that part of
his growing-up experience was to discuss theology with
teachers of the law.

This passage is followed by another; one which covers
18 years of sinless development and preparation.

> Then he went down to Nazareth with them and was obedient
> to them. But his mother treasured all these things in her heart.
> And Jesus grew in wisdom and stature, and in favour with
> God and men. (Luke 2:51–52)

Consider this throw-away summation of his teenage years:
he 'was obedient to them'. Of course, we believe it because
we believe Jesus lived a life of sinless perfection, which

qualified him to be the perfect sacrifice for our sin. But please just pause for a moment and allow the impact of the word 'obedient' to sink in. Obedient through the teenage years which are characterised for everyone else by rebellion, sexual awakening, conflict, struggles with authority and rules and curfews, and flawed, exasperating parents . . . Jesus survived this part of life not only without sin, but also in a way which prepared him for his ministry.

He grew in four areas: intellectually (wisdom); physically (stature); spiritually (favour with God) and socially (favour with men). This is so crucial! Let's learn early to minister to the whole person.

The next scene where Christ demonstrates his self-discipline is in the wilderness, fasting for forty days and nights and then being directly challenged by the devil himself (Luke 4:1–13). Jesus considers each temptation in terms of scriptures he has memorised. How many scriptures have you memorised? And how many of those are ones which directly apply to temptations you face? There's an immediate benefit to being self-disciplined in terms of Scripture memorisation.

Jesus not only sidesteps these temptations; he doesn't get angry or frustrated either. Some of us get cranky if we miss out on elevenses, let alone forty days and forty nights of fasting. Six weeks without mealtimes leaves anyone in a weakened state; apart from the obvious physical impact, the depleted blood-sugar levels in the brain can make a big difference to moods. Formerly easy-going, cheerful, righteous people become awkward, snappy and, frankly, far less pious than usual. But Jesus dealt with the conflict directly.

Forty days without food meant that bread was a very desirable commodity. But he knew his life was bound up with God, and that he should not use his miraculous powers for his own gratification.

These gruelling forty days of preparation for his ministry meant that the offer of authority and power immediately, without the work or the cross, must have been almost compelling. But Jesus' self-discipline gave him the strength to quote a commandment that refuted the claims of the evil one.

And Jesus was facing a long, hard road of conflict and disbelief about his identity, so the offer of immediate recognition as the Son of God, borne up in the air by angels, must have been giddyingly attractive. The devil certainly knows how to tempt! But Jesus stood firm, knowing that testing God does not honour him.

The direct assault on Jesus was a failure; so the devil went off to stir up hatred and unbelief and negativism and hardness of heart in the religious leaders, the authorities and most of the people of Galilee and Judea, in his attempts to defeat Jesus. All he had to achieve was to goad him into one sin; but the self-discipline of Jesus was tough.

> For we do not have a high priest who is unable to sympathise with our weaknesses, but we have one who has been tempted in every way, just as we are – yet was without sin. (Hebrews 4:15)

Jesus was without sin; Jesus has been tempted in every one of the ways in which we are tempted; Jesus sympathises.

But note that he has also resisted temptations we won't ever have to face. The devil tempts us to turn money into cream cakes, not stones into bread. The devil tempts us to dream of authority and splendour, but we know we don't deserve it, unlike Jesus, who did deserve it. And the devil usually tempts us to misunderstand or deny our identity rather than prove it.

There are many other incidents in the life of Christ where we can observe self-discipline at work. He walked through the crowd that wanted to throw him down a cliff (see Luke 4:28–30). I'd have become slightly agitated. He showed grace when the Pharisees began to whisper darkly about him (Luke 5:21–25). I'd have ground my teeth. He answered coolly and wisely when the Pharisees challenged his attitude to the Sabbath (Luke 6:1–11). I'd have offered the (withered or unwithered) five-fold knuckle sandwich of fellowship to the lot of them.

And so on. His challenges never overstepped into sneers. His direct attacks on the Pharisees never became rude personal accusations. His willingness to confront never deteriorated into slanging matches. His defence against false testimony, lies and injustice was silently to submit to the authorities, knowing that he was doing the will of God as he went to the cross.

He set his face towards Jerusalem and the destiny he had agreed with the Father way back when they created the world. But he was still exercising discipline as he prayed in Gethsemane, with sweat like great drops of blood. Discipline isn't just not sinning; it's active, hard-work righteousness, too.

TO CONSIDER

1. How many children can you name who can be described as strong, wise and gracious? Do you think it's fair to use Jesus as a comparison?
2. What are the direct results of resisting temptation?

9. Reflect on What You Expect

What standard of behaviour do you expect from the children or young people in your care? And do those expectations need to be adjusted?

It is reasonable to expect that little children will do as they are told, because that is the standard to which they have become accustomed. Parents take a responsible role and provide guidance on what is advisable, preferred, demanded, etc. For instance, 'No!' is often the first word a little baby learns to say, because it is the word most often said to them, as they taste dirt, investigate gas fires, prod little friends in the eye or tinker with electric sockets. Responsible parenting demands that the child's natural curiosity is tempered with adult wisdom, to protect the child from being harmed or causing harm to others. It would be a nuisance to everyone else if your child shorted out the national grid, for example.

As children grow older, it is appropriate for them to develop independence, and for this to result in experiment

69

and learning through experience, not just living according to the rules. 'Why?' they may ask. 'Ow!' comes the rapid reply, when they discover that the reason to keep away from the gas fire is because too much heat hurts.

Children turn into young teens very quickly, and what was simply disobedience at age eight may very well turn into resentful disrespect by the onset of the teenage years.

I agree, it doesn't have to be that way. There are some families where the children are thoroughly prepared by their parents for the changes which are about to happen. Armed with this information, the youngsters make a much more smooth transition into adolescence and beyond.

CASE STUDY: PASSIONATE PRAY-ER

Ralph loved the Lord from an early age, and as he grew up, his love deepened and matured. A witty, cheerful, articulate lad, he was a regular volunteer and a consistent encouragement. He became a teenager and became stronger in God. His passion for the lost was focused on two or three of the guys in his class, and when one of them, Simon, became a regular member of the youth group, no one could have been more delighted than Ralph. Time passed, and Simon still had made no expression of faith. Ralph prayed with great earnestness (sometimes with tears) and cried out to God for the soul of his pal. When the evening came that Simon prayed for salvation, it was hard for Ralph to contain his joy and relief!

Ralph's parents had found a happy medium between laid-back and hands-on, and had steered Ralph without railroading him. He felt that each was both approachable and deeply respected; he shared friendship with his parents as well as sonship.

It wasn't just good luck; Ralph's younger sister also sailed confidently and maturely through adolescence and has grown into a young woman who demonstrates a love for God and a healthy attitude to gaining independence.

In both cases, they were given full warnings of the onslaught they were about to face before the physical and psychological changes started.

I cannot recommend highly enough *Preparing for Adolescence* by Dr James Dobson, who writes with clarity and affection about young people, explaining how parents can help youngsters find their way through this essential but painful time of life.

In many ways, we can demonstrate to the children and young people what we expect of them by the way we have provided for their physical needs. Imagine these scenes . . .

Expect the worst

You're aged seven, and you walk into the church building down a shadowy side alley. The door is stiff, and you have to push hard to get it to open, and as you do, you notice that one of the bulbs in the hallway has blown, and the other is failing to illumine the space. You happen to know that your meeting is through the second door on the left, and you go into the room. The silence is almost as deafening as the cold dampness is clammy; the carpet is old, a bit threadbare and not that clean. There are stacks of chairs around the wall. You are among the first of the children to arrive, and the box of dressing-up clothes has been strewn all over the floor by young Jimmy Smith, the two-year-old son of one of the helpers. Mrs Smith is pinning a flower rota on the notice-board, and doesn't notice that you have come in. Mrs Jones is also here, but she's fussing with a table and some cut-out bits of paper, so she doesn't notice that you've arrived, either. You lean against the wall, and watch Jimmy for a while, as he tries on a hat or two. After a short while, three other children arrive. One of them is your friend, so you have a conversation, comparing your most recently acquired scars on your knees. The other children are arriving, and the noise levels in the room are rising and Mrs Smith turns and 'shush'es vigorously. It's the first time today she's acknowledged your presence, and it's clear she's cross already.

Expect the best

You're aged seven, and you bounce out of the car when you see the big sign hung over the bright yellow door to the church. It's a friendly welcome, as well as confirmation that you've come to the right place. At the door is that nice Mary, who smiles when she sees you and greets you by name, asking how your mum is, and wondering if you enjoyed the trip to the theme park you were excitedly telling her about last week. You go inside through the propped-open door into the warm room with the bright sign. Sally is here, and smiles at you as she chats with several other children, who are crowding around her. The posters on the wall are large and colourful (one of them is a map, and the other three are of children playing). The carpet is soft and spongy and smells nice. There are three other helpers: Helen, a teenage girl; Big Dave, who told everyone last week about his job as a fireman; and Sally, who is one of the dinnerladies at your school. All of the adults were ready when you came in, and they are all nice, in your opinion. You chat with other children, and then Sally claps her hands gently to get attention, and she explains the first game.

Which scene do you prefer? Which scene is more like the way children enter your meetings week by week? Are they made to feel welcome in a friendly, child-oriented environment, which has been prepared ahead of time with care and appropriate materials? Or is it as if it's a drab, cheerless, second-best minor irritation in the schedule of the busy, distracted, not-yet-ready people who appear to be making an effort to put up with you and your little friends?

OK, these extremes have been included to make a point, but it is my firmly held belief that courtesy demands that we are ready for the arrival of the children or young people at the time they are due to arrive. Our practice is to be ready a few minutes earlier than that, so we can discuss any special activities we are planning, and take the opportunity to pray together. This means that when the arrival time strikes, we are there, prepared, and able to do what we are there for – to meet, greet and make relationships with the youngsters. The quality of the carpet and the decoration of the room can make a real difference to the attitude of the children, but the attitude of the children's workers is fundamental.

A good start sets the tone for the event; if you give the impression that you'd prefer the children to be elsewhere, then they will probably respond likewise. By the time you get to your well-prepared, lively, visual talk on a relevant topic, you may find that the rest of the message you have been delivering has had a negative effect on enthusiastic participation in your session.

The proof of the padding . . .

. . . is, of course, in the seating. Opinion is divided on the use of chairs.

Chairs can make the room feel formal, which is not desirable, but ordered, which is. Having insufficient chairs is simply unfair on latecomers, who are probably not the ones responsible for their arrival time. Seating children on shaggy or threadbare carpets is unwise, as anyone not wearing jeans or trousers will have their legs tickled by the shaggy pile, or become fidgety very quickly by the lack of comfort.

When someone goes to the trouble of providing a chair for me, I feel that my presence is welcomed and expected. I can relax and focus on the topic, rather than being distracted by being uncomfortable or by 'pins and needles' in my legs. I am also given a space to occupy when I have a chair; sitting on the floor is less precise, less ordered and much more likely to encourage 'lolling' or leaning or other forms of childlike interference from other parties.

Having uncomfortable chairs is making the worst of both worlds.

Proper preparation prevents poor performance

That's not always true, but the principle is a sound one. If I'm unready for the session, then I can only really expect a poor presentation, which is shortchanging the youngsters. I'll be fumbling through my props, unsure of the running order, unable to inspire my team, unclear in the instructions I give for games, or time of prayer, or response. I certainly won't give off an air of confident authority. OK, so we all know that even when I give off an air of confident authority I'm like the proverbial duck, purposeful and elegant on the surface, but paddling like fury underneath! On the other hand, I can testify that when I feel prepared and focused on my topic, I can perform in a relaxed and cheerful way. This is something I cannot achieve when I'm panicking about what comes next, or if I've written down the Bible references correctly, or if my theology checks out, or any other problem.

My suggestion is to take heed of what the Scripture says.

Each day has enough trouble of its own. (Matthew 6:34)

My personal application of this verse is to make sure that *everything* I could do beforehand, I do beforehand. That means I am free to react to the unexpected incident, interruption, question or heckling which may occur during the session, and for which I cannot prepare. If I turn up unready, then that just adds to what I shall have to achieve while on my feet, and there is, believe me, a limit to this. I need to concentrate on what I am saying, not on worries such as: 'Have we remembered to buy more orange squash?' or: 'Why have I written Mark 17:11 in these notes, since there are only 16 chapters in Mark?' I'd rather have those wrinkles ironed out before I stand up in front of the little ones.

Now this is not to exclude the surprising or spontaneous activity of the Holy Spirit, which is to be welcomed at all sessions. Adjustments which are required as a result of his presence in the session can be made as you go along, and should be allowed for and earnestly prayed for at the preparation stage. That means you should always have at least one item you can joyfully drop to make time for spontaneous supernatural phenomena.

Who's expecting what?

It's not just the expectation of a good time in the eyes of the children; and it's not just your expectation of the session. Another key person in the way God has established our spiritual relationships is the overseer. In other words, who's in charge of the people in charge?

You'll probably agree with me that human nature dictates that if you know you're going to be checked, you'll revise more. And so it is when you know the pastor will be standing at the back, listening to your children's talk; this will give you the impetus to polish it.

Now, of course we all know that Jesus is standing there

listening, knowing all the time we 'wing it', or 'fly by the seat of our pants', or 'get away with it', having been careless, or even lazy, in our preparation. But when there is a member of the church leadership team, or a deacon, or the children's work superintendent present, making sure that standards of excellence in style and content are being maintained, this concentrates the mind beautifully. This is caring, helpful, approachable oversight and accountability.

For a number of years, I have submitted to a mentoring system within church life, which provides me with a so-called 'partner for growth'. In my case, this is a Scottish schoolteacher who supports Derby County and enjoys a glass of wine as he practises generous hospitality. He is a mature Christian who is committed to praying for me, to meeting with me on a regular basis to encourage and strengthen me, as well as being someone with whom demonstrating vulnerability or distress is not interpreted as weakness. My role is to provide the same for him, and it works!

He tells me when the pressure's on in the staff room or in his finances, and I call him when I feel the need for encouragement or wisdom. Discussing his marriage is (by mutual consent) 'off-limits', but he's been known to mention the names of a few of the nubile womenfolk in the church in whom he suggests I might take an interest (I'm not complaining!).

Neither of us is 'the one who must be obeyed'; it's not that sort of a relationship. But when he comes to the youth club to play the guitar excellently for our worship time,

I make sure that my involvement is similarly polished and prepared.

You may feel this amounts to performing to impress each other, but who loses out? Certainly not the young people, as they are blessed with a good session from both of us. OK, so maybe we should be so good every time that we don't need to do this; but the reality is that there are good moments and weaker aspects to any long-term ministry. I'd rather be good most weeks and excellent on some occasions than let the standard gradually deteriorate. So I'm exercising self-discipline in order to reap the reward of well-taught and well-entertained young people, focused on the topic, with few distractions and discipline problems.

Expect to be worth hearing

As mentioned before (Chapter 6), make sure that the teaching style used provides sufficient interest for the youngsters to hold their attention on the topic. But think of this: you have the words of eternal life, full of grace and truth, with wonderful, life-enhancing stories and adventures. They are penned through the inspiration of the Holy Spirit, and peopled by godly men and women setting examples worth following or learning from as they face trials and troubles, their own weaknesses and the mighty power of God indwelling them daily. What a privilege to be handling this material! What a glorious calling, to instruct the young in the ways of God!

Schoolteachers have to achieve the same goals with topics such as physics or, even worse, French. These are, by definition, non-eternal, as all earthly things will pass away.

> Do your best to present yourself to God as one approved, a
> workman who does not need to be ashamed and who cor-
> rectly handles the word of truth. (2 Timothy 2:15)

If you expect to be worth hearing, and your expectations
are realistic and measurable, then this will probably raise
your game.

By this I am suggesting that you could ask a colleague to
give you a critique on the session, emphasising good
points more than mistakes, but being realistic about the
weak or out-of-control moments. Someone who loves you
(and the youngsters) enough to do this is rare but very
precious.

High standards set corporately

Helping young people understand that the rules will be
applied fairly and consistently by all team members is
vital. One 'too-friendly' team member can undermine (or
at least confuse) the message the rest of you are trying to
communicate. In his efforts to be friendly and approachable, he is in fact setting a poor example by chatting or
whispering at the wrong times, or permitting behaviour
that should not be allowed.

One of the most successful efforts we have made to help
the young people feel truly members of the youth group
(not just attendees) is to include them in the rule-setting
process.

The young people themselves have agreed the basic rules of the club, thus:

- Treat the building, equipment, team members and club members with respect.
- Leave the light switches alone.
- Don't leave the building during the evening unless accompanied by a team member.
- Remember to go to the loo before the power hour.

These 'dos and don'ts' have good reasons behind them. For example, innocent young people may not realise that drunks may ring the church door bell on a Saturday night, perhaps expecting handouts, and it's best to allow an adult to deal with this. There is slightly less disruption to the meeting if at least some have spent a penny beforehand. Slightly. But why build in a disruption when by mutual consent you can try to eliminate it?

Having established the wisdom and mutual benefit of these rules gives us a firm foundation on which to stand when youngsters are discovered redhandedly destroying badminton rackets, or attempting to cause a flood by filling toilet bowls with tissue, or getting up to any other of their hilarious(?) pranks.

TO CONSIDER

1. What standard of behaviour do you expect from the children or young people in your care? Do those expectations need to be adjusted?

2. Think about your meetings from the child's viewpoint. Are they welcoming? Are you ready? Is the first interaction between child and adult positive or negative?

3. What lessons can be learned from the times when you've started the children's meeting underprepared?

10. You're the Adult!

While high expectations of behaviour could very well result in higher standards being achieved, there will always be lapses, mistakes, challenges and disobedience. Children and young people run in corridors, pick at slight imperfections in the paintwork, shout, twiddle with curtains, act irresponsibly and challenge authority; they do all the things you don't want them to do. They even find things to do that you didn't know were things you didn't want them to do. That's what they do. They behave like children or like young people, and we love them for it, even though we desire to shape their behaviour by instructing them about appropriate attitudes.

But through it all, we are the adults. The responsibility for the safety and enjoyment of the event is with us. Always consider the good of the many over the fun or exuberance or disobedience of the few.

CASE STUDY: CHATTING TO CHARLIE

One of the nicest, wittiest, grown-up lads we have ever had in the youth group went through a short phase where his attitude was less than appropriate. Charlie seemed to have a negative opinion about many of the things we had thought he liked. He was vocal in his criticism of the way the club was run, and he refused to obey some of the rules. He made snide remarks about team members and other young people. He started to use his size to his advantage with some of the smaller boys and he certainly over-emphasised his importance as the son of a church leader.

Eventually, we had to make a decision. Should we permit this sort of rebellion to continue, making allowances for the fact that church leaders' offspring have a much harder time than many other youngsters? Two of the three youth group leaders had personal experience of this. My considered view was that the enemy of souls wishes to find many ways to drive a wedge between church leaders and their flock. When children's and youth workers have cause to criticise their elders and pastors on account of the bad behaviour of their kids, Satan's goal is, in part, achieved. Or should we exercise authority, asking Charlie, a church leader's son, to obey our rules, just like anyone else?

In the end, we confronted Charlie's poor attitude and behaviour, and found that his father supported us to the hilt, despite his surprise at the recent deterioration of Charlie's pleasantness. Being confronted for having a poor attitude rarely helps someone gain a better attitude, but eventually we saw a change in his approach. Later in life, he may recognise that we were trying to help shape his development, not just punish him for a few off-beat remarks and incidents.

This was a positive result; not all are so encouraging . . .

CASE STUDY: JUMPING ON JIM

*The extreme anger of one young man named **Jim** led him into a punch-up with Phil, one of our team members. I know Phil should have turned the other cheek and all that, but in the heat of the moment he turned away in self-protection (not a bad idea, even if it's not the best idea). Sadly, Jim thought this was a good chance to get in another punch, and the two chaps ended up on the floor. Phil was trying to protect himself, and Jim was trying to knock seven bells out of Phil.*

Observing this, Russ (another of the leaders) and I made the decision that Jim would have to leave the building, so we asked him to do so. He refused to comply, so we approached him in a way he interpreted as threatening, and reacted violently. In the end, Jim was ejected and invited to return at a later date, but not before he landed several more blows on Russ and me, and indeed on the hapless Phil. It wasn't the most successful of persuasions. I was asked afterwards how I felt about this failure; I tried to see it in positive terms and spoke glowingly of all the young people who were rescued from an angry young man who lost his temper. When he was sadly ejected from the building, the evening returned to one which was peaceful and safe.

But I was only half-convinced that I'd done the right thing. Was it an appropriate response to his violent behaviour to be confrontational? Could I have tried to calm the emotional situation in another way? Probably. But in the heat of the moment, I acted in a way that had the best chance of defusing the danger to everyone else (especially the bruised and battered Phil), even if that procedure could have resulted in danger to myself.

The over-riding principle which applies here is that we are the adults and should be the ones to act responsibly. Threatening or violent reactions are just as hopeless as the poor behaviour which incites them. It is not our place to lose our temper. Our policy is to always ensure that two team leaders become involved when poor behaviour is being confronted. This protects everyone from anger, reaction or accusation.

Lean on the rules

If you have agreed and well-publicised rules to lean upon, you may feel free to do so! But if the youngsters are confused about what is permitted and what is not, then it is unfair to expect them to obey the rules. Impetuous or inconsistent application of unwritten rules just winds people up. But clearly stated and consistently applied rules make everyone aware of the perimeters of their freedom.

Consider the extent of the rules, and decide which of them are fundamental. The youthful irresponsibility of forgetting to go to the loo before the meeting starts is not a serious offence. Consistently sneaking off to the loo during the meeting to have a crafty smoke is an act of disobedience and is serious; nipping out in order wilfully to damage church property must be discouraged very firmly.

What about the accidentally broken window? Some children take this very seriously, as they have been taught to do so at home. Dad may regard the breaking of a window as a serious offence, since he has established a domestic rule about not kicking a ball near the house.

But when a stray shot flies off the crossbar of the goal and smashes an unprotected window in the church hall, my response is threefold. I reassure the youngster that I agree it was 'just an accident', I clear up the glass immediately and I let the caretaker know that a replacement window is required, please. There was no malicious act of deliberately attempting to damage the window; it could have happened to anyone. The risk of breakage was accepted when the hall was made available for football. That's why we have invested in shatterproof sheets of clear plastic to guard all the windows, which means we can play all sorts of ball games in the hall. But some shots are so powerful that accidents happen. It goes with the territory.

Confronting

When pointing out rule infringements, I have discovered that continually to appeal to the reason of the youngster and the reasonableness of my comments can keep the issue from escalating into World War Three. I have also learned to restate the rule and stick to it, rather than use an approach which is more accusing. For example, I say quietly: 'Steve, that's a cue, not a weapon,' and he is then free to assert the rule about treating the equipment with respect himself. The choice is his, and has not been appropriated by me as the enforcer.

Or I may have to say 'Steve [yes, use their name so they know that you know them and that you mean them, not someone else], you're not loitering in the corridor, are you?'

'No,' he says, going into one of the supervised rooms.

'Didn't think so,' I say, as I continue on my way. Good result. Steve's in a room, having decided to make the move rather than actively confront the rule, and no one's told anyone off. Lovely!

Or it may be more serious.

'Steve, what's the rule about the way you should treat the building?'

'Er, sorry.'

'No, I meant what's the rule?'

'Don't damage it.'

'That is true. So what are you sorry about?' (Encourage the sinner to acknowledge his sin.)

'I tore the wallpaper. It was already a bit torn, and I just tore it some more. I didn't mean to, it just sort of . . . happened. Franko and Dazzer were there, too and they did it a bit.'

'OK. I'll talk to them as well. But what do you think we should be doing about it?'

'What do you mean?'

'Er, well, who do you think would be the right person to pay something towards the repairs?'

'Me and Franko and Dazzer.'

'I think I agree with you. Do you think that would be fair?'

'I suppose so.'

'OK, well, that's what I'll recommend to the people in charge of maintenance, and we'll get back to you when we know how much money we're talking about. Is that all right then, Steve? Do you think I'm being reasonable?'

'Yes. Sorry.'

'I accept your apology; I don't expect you'll do it again, and I hope you won't be upset when you find out how much it will cost.'

The confrontation is thus conducted in a reasonably adult way, and both parties feel that their views have been heard. I wouldn't admit it to Steve at this point, but I feel that the maintenance department should take some of the responsibility if there was already damage or loose paper; it's simply an invitation to pick at it if it's loose. When the estimate for repairs is presented, I expect Steve and his pals (or, to be more realistic, their parents) won't have to pay it all.

We are called to be like Christ and show love and forgiveness to those who break the rules. We may also correct them, as long as we use gentleness, grace and mercy, not just judgement and wrath. They may not be in a frame of mind to receive correction, but they need to know that they are valued and have worth.

'You're a nice kid, but I can't put up with tonight's behaviour, mate!'

'You may not have realised it, but several people were frightened and some were in danger when you got angry like that.'

'One of the rules is that you show respect to the team members; you were rude to Sophie, and she's one of the team, so that's not acceptable. Am I being unreasonable?'

'It's the same rule for everyone, so I'm not just picking on you . . .'

My understanding of young people tells me that they

usually respond to reasonableness more than to anger or lectures. So I try to curb anger or verbal diarrhoea (I'm sometimes able to supply both, simultaneously, and it's not nice) and just calmly explain my understanding of the rules, the infringements and the penalties. All of these are publicly explained at the start of each academic year, and publicly displayed during each youth club meeting. I make it a personal rule never to end the conversation without asking the question: 'Am I being fair?', waiting for a response and then discussing any dissenting thoughts. I want to be reasonable, and I find that most young teens can be reasoned with, and appreciate that I go out of my way to be fair.

TO CONSIDER

1. In what ways should church leaders' children be treated differently?
2. What is your attitude to accidental damage?
3. How can you add grace and compassion to your confrontations? Or, how can you add discipline and firmness to your kindness and indulgence?

11. Two Different Models

The first of these helpful styles of approaching discipline is proposed by the most excellent Dr James Dobson in his bestseller *Dare to Discipline*.

Reward good behaviour

First of all, we need to tackle the divisive question of the natural state of children. Are they clean slates, ready to be taught rightousness and good ways to relate to one another? Or are they thoroughly wicked, with an in-built propensity toward sinning?

Whichever of these views is the one to which you subscribe (basically good or basically bad), you'll quickly discover that babies are selfish, lazy, demanding and ungrateful. They need to be taught to be good, to say 'please' and 'thank you' and to refrain from throwing spoonfuls of beef and carrot purée over Grandma. Their responsibility for their actions is disputed; some say babies cannot reason and so they are not responsible. Others say they are unable to reason, but their sinful nature is showing through in sinful behaviour. No one is suggesting that punishment is appropriate at this stage, probably.

Anyway, the bottom line is that young children need to be encouraged to do the good things and to be discouraged from doing wrong things. Dr Dobson is keen to instruct us to reward good behaviour.

The children's workers who stand at the front, arms folded, waiting for silence from all, are failing to put this principle into practice; they are punishing the obedient, quiet children, while the chatterers carry on. When the children notice what's happening, they may fall silent out of guilt. In summary, the good children are punished and the naughty or distracted ones have a nice chat. Something wrong here, surely? And it doesn't wash to argue that the quiet ones ought to be quiet since that's the norm or standard of behaviour required. They are obeying the rules and they shouldn't be punished for it.

A successful, practical outworking of the principle of rewarding – and thus reinforcing – good or preferred behaviour within your children's church meetings could be a star chart. This is nothing to do with astrology, but a means of rewarding such good behaviours as: 'Cleaned up after the craft activity'; 'Remembered to bring a Bible'; 'Among the first to be quiet when asked'; 'Quoted the memory verse without needing a prompt'; and 'Listened well this morning'. A child would quickly learn that when they behave well, they are rewarded. They like the reward, so they make sure that next time, they offer the reward-earning behaviour. But beware! They will lose interest when they discover that the children's leader thinks the stars themselves are a reward. No, no; the stars should be a way of adding up towards a prize worth having, such as sweets, a trip to McDonald's, extra ice-creams during the outing, or other quantifiable goodies.

Bribery, I hear you whispering to yourself, in case Dr Dobson overhears. But he's already thought of that. Reward systems are riddled through our adult lives. For example, you don't go to work for the good of the firm, or just for something to do, do you? No, the company realises it has to acknowledge your work with a pay cheque every month. Soldiers are rewarded not just with pay – and not just with the joy of knowing they fought for freedom, or for the honour of their country, either (*'dulce et decorum est'*, and all that). Those who perform exceptionally receive medals as well.

So if it's OK for adults, then it's hypocrisy for us to complain about it being applied to children, right? Affirm the well-behaved whenever you can, and they might (just might) supply similar behaviour next time.

Punish bad behaviour

Now we come to the controversial bit. Dr Dobson advocates the administration of punishment for children who step out of line. That's OK, and most of what he suggests is sound counsel. But when he starts to suggest corporal punishment, and even gives directions on how to hurt to the max without leaving a mark, I have to stop and think carefully, since there is something distinctly unpleasant about this.

Two specific problems occur to me. First, it is against the law for me to use corporal punishment on any children not my own. The Social Contract and the Maastricht Treaty look like continuously eroding at choices parents can make in terms of smacking their children, but the Children Act protects all youngsters from physical punishment from church children's and youth workers.

Secondly, my observations of children and young people tell me that it is only after careful analysis of each individual that I can tell what strength of admonition is appropriate. Sam chats when required to listen, but he does not respond to anything except being reprimanded with the force of a nuclear explosion. Meanwhile, Katie has once or twice been found to be not paying attention; she blushes and withers at anything stronger than a look with a smile.

In the light of this, 'clips around the ear' are doubly off-limits; I'm opening myself up to prosecution, and I may be massively over-reacting to a sensitive child.

I agree that poor behaviour needs a response; fast, decisive and unpleasant. But a society ruled by violence leads to a society where violence is tolerated, and that cannot be right.

So, you may be asking, what is permissible? What measures or sanctions can be used to mould behaviour, or as a reminder of the consequences of law-breaking?

In the same way as pleasant rewards reinforce good behaviour, the withdrawal of the things the child desires can be used to teach him to stay within the rules. For example, take Mike and Greg, two eight-year-old boys who sit and talk when they should be listening. You are not up at the front, but are part of the 'sit among the kids and help them to listen' team. They clearly want to talk and you want them to be quiet and to listen. You have four goals:

1. that they cease chatting
2. that they remain quiet
3. that they listen
4. that they dislike the punishment for breaking the rule.

Now, it seems to me that if you politely ask them to be quiet, you have communicated adequately your preferred behaviour, even though it's a standard house rule. If they continue to chat (90 per cent chance) you might ask them to be quiet, reminding them that it's a rule. If they still continue (70 per cent, after a short spell of quiet), move Greg to another part of the room, and sit him next to you.

What have you achieved? Goals 1, 2 and 4. Getting them to listen is the responsibility of the person telling the story, who now has a much better chance of success, because Greg and Mike are no longer talking to each other, and because the distraction for the other children has been removed, too.

The 'divide and conquer' technique is simple but very effective. No eight-year-old boy like Greg wants to sit with you ('boring'), so you have given him a good reason to avoid chatting with Mike next time, as he knows you'll be consistent and fair about repeating the punishment. I have even seen habitual chatterers deliberately sit away from their friends in order to spare themselves the unpleasantness of having to be moved to a spot they dislike, next to a team member.

The schoolteacher's job, when you get right down to it, is to provide lessons where various subjects can be learned. But our calling and task are much more than this. We are not paid to 'get through the lesson' (we are not paid, most of us!) but rather we desire to communicate and impart spiritual truth to the hearts of these youngsters, so sending persistent offenders out of the room is tempting, but not an option. Better indeed to examine why they offend: are they bored? Have we not provided a forum for them to chat? Do they not understand the rules? Are we expecting them to give attention for longer than they can manage?

CASE STUDY: IT CAN'T BE DONE

Alan, a hyperactive young man, much preferred sports and larks to singing or listening. But having sat him down, we succeeded in getting his flighty attention onto a topic which interested him. All well and good. However, Alan's learned pattern of behaviour in the formal setting soon returned and he lost the new-found co-operation after ten minutes, and reverted to being disruptive, chatty, and shouting out silly comments.

Lessons we learned the hard way: even when you get everything right, you've only got it right for a few minutes. We rested on laurels, and ended up with crushed leaves.

So what's the other method?

It seems much harder to achieve, but is much more rewarding and has superb long-term implications. Rather than rewarding good behaviour and punishing bad behaviour, this approach expects good behaviour all the time. What?

The thinking behind this is that children need attention and love and encouragement. So if parents provide this to the point that children understand that they are loved, accepted, valued and respected, they will respond on the whole with obedience, love, and a desire to do what is expected. This is based on a theology of God's grace, which points out that we cannot please God, or make him love us more, since he already loves us to the utmost. Our desire to do his will is not based on a primitive 'pleasing the gods lest their anger burn against us' denial of the power of the cross of Christ. I am a son of God through the shed blood of Jesus; my salvation is secure and my sonship eternal.

So this is worked out by consistently giving the child love and attention until the child has received enough to run by himself for a little while. I believe this is referred to as 'filling up his love tank', like a fuel tank in a car. After the tank is filled, the car or child can get on with life knowing they are loved, and knowing what is expected of them. After a while, the child returns for more fuel.

The contrast is strong. The first method assumes the child will be bad, so it encourages good behaviour and punishes the inevitable bad behaviour. But this other approach seems to try to 'head bad behaviour off at the pass'; to short-circuit it, if you will, by eliminating the need for attention-seeking of any kind.

The children's worker uses the second model when designing a meeting that is gung-ho from the start – there is so much going on in short bursts that attention is constantly being grabbed and held, there's no time for larks, and kids have no need to make their own fun.

Conclusion

Both of these philosophical approaches to discipline have been constructed with primarily the parent and child at home in mind, and not for the specific challenges of the church context. We have a large child to adult ratio; much less consistency (1–2 hours' contact a week, rather than 12–16 hours a day). In addition, and far more importantly, the children and young people are influenced most of their lives by their parents' choice of disciplinary styles (or lack of same). In other words, it is almost immaterial how much you reinforce good behaviour or punish bad behaviour if the message the child has learned at home is that they can get away with nearly anything most of the time, but pay for it with the occasional clobbering. Or if they have learned that they are worthless, sinful scum, expected to be thoroughly wicked, they will probably do all they can to live up to this reputation!

The reality is that children's and youth workers have to deal with a hotchpotch of disciplinary styles. Some have been successful, but many more have not, and the children are confused, and the young people are perhaps even angry and rebellious. We cannot expect to bring about change instantly. But children will quickly learn to deliver if we make sure they know what we expect and reward.

TO CONSIDER

1. Which of the two models best describes the approach you prefer?
2. What are the merits of rewarding or acknowledging good behaviour?
3. Which children in your care respond only to strong rebukes, and which respond to merely a gentle look?

12. Suggested Techniques

So, we've now considered the nature and nurture of the children in your care, and the differing qualities and effectiveness of the way their parents view and treat them.

One of the most delightful, rewarding and downright hard work aspects of children and youth work is prayer.

On your knees

We've got this close to the end of the book and we still haven't found a single Bible reference to Sunday school, children's workers or bouncing praise, let alone other 'fundamental' elements of church life, such as housegroup, curates or inexpressible inward joy. But nevertheless, we believe in most of these things, so I shall continue moving gently on. Joking apart, children's and youth workers can be evangelists, pastors or deacons (practical servants), so I am convinced that there is an appropriate role for us to play – none more so than the essential service of prayer.

It is very appropriate for those who care for the flock of God to speak to him about them, before speaking to them about him. This does not mean five snatched minutes' prayer before the little ones arrive; my feeling is that prayer should characterise our dealings with them. Pray for them daily. Some of them may have grandmothers and parents who pray for them regularly, and you can join your prayers with the prayers of these saints. Other children may rarely be the subject of tender requests left at the throne of grace, especially those from unbelieving households. Perhaps all they get is curses, not blessings. So we can have a significant involvement in their lives (one which they may never know about, or only discover years later). What a privilege!

Pray for the children and young people when you meet as a team of workers. Whether this is once a month or more often, prayer should be on the agenda. Maybe your team of workers doesn't meet this often; I suggest you should, even if only to pray for the children. Name them before God and make requests for their spiritual growth and development. Pray for those who are part of dysfunctional families, but be careful to preserve the dignity and/or privacy of parents. Call on God to pour out his grace and peace on the naughty ones. Thank God for blessing your group with these children.

Praying for children and young people will have at least two effects: God will be requested to bless them and save them and assist them in righteousness, and your attitude towards them will be softened and made more gracious. I have found that it's really hard to pray for a child who is annoying, and that it's really hard to get annoyed with someone for whom you are regularly praying.

So if Olly or DJ or Vicki winds you up and makes you cross, why not add them to your prayer list and call upon the throne of God to pour blessing down on them? Who knows what massive good this might do?

> A gentle answer turns away wrath, but a harsh word stirs up anger. (Proverbs 15:1)

I am convinced that this Bible verse has enormous power. It would seem that childish disobedience and youthful rebellion need to be met with equal force, but actually our calm adult confidence and wisdom are dynamite!

Where, oh where?

Exercise caution when disciplining a child or young person. Remember that they are a person too, and while you may dislike or need to curtail their behaviour, their dignity or reputation may be at stake. Consider the reasons behind their naughtiness or rebellion, and please don't just wade in there with all guns blazing.

Belittling show-offs is tempting, especially when they are disrupting your session with silliness and antics. I am tempted to use the put-down 'Grow up!' when this happens, but I try not to yield to this. If trying to gain attention when I'm up at the front, I usually appeal to courtesy, or make polite requests for them to look and listen.

'One of the rules is that you should not be distracting others, Billy.'

'Please don't make that noise; I'm finding that rather off-putting, old chap.'

'Please stop talking, you two.'

'Enough now, thank you. I don't want to have to ask you again . . .'

'Sophie, will you please separate Kelly and Mary-Anne, because they are continually chattering.'

Other phrases sometimes heard in our meetings (although not necessarily recommended):

'Button it!'

'Pack it in!'

'I grow weary of having to ask you to give me your attention.'

'Simon Foster, shut your mouth!' High levels of exasperation are reached all too quickly.

Sometimes these gentle appeals to courtesy work, but only when what I have to say or show is interesting and worth their attention. I won't get attention unless I'm interesting. I certainly don't deserve attention if my negative or aggressive attitude denies what I am trying to say about the forgiving love of God.

Private conversations

But a much better way of disciplining a child or a young person is to do so privately. This does not mean getting out of sight of other children or adults, as that has an appearance of evil, which is equally unhelpful.

Do you remember the old TV show from the sixties *Not in Front of the Children*? Of course you don't; you're far too youthful. But believe me, there was one. It was a family sitcom, and the main theme was that when the parents disagreed they had to remember to keep their discussions out of the sight of their offspring. Or something equally hilarious. Oh yes, TV was grim in the olden days.

Anyway, taking a child to one side to have a calm conversation respects his dignity while giving him no reason to show-off or continue to seek the attention of the other children. In public, you are mostly limited to being critical of the naughtiness. But in private, you can ask if he's feeling OK, or if there is some other reason why he has been misbehaving; perhaps you have inside information about home life or a recent incident which may be on his mind. Taking the young person to one side gives you the chance to minister to him, not just to exercise authority over him.

But what if?

When my role is to be in the crowd and keep order, I will try to be proactive in setting a good example. This means that I face the front and refrain from making conversation, no matter how tempting the circumstances. I will make clear my disapproval of chatting going on around me, and try to keep order effectively.

It can be complicated to keep changing roles, but there comes a time when I have to be the policeman, even if earlier in the clubnight or Sunday meeting I've been the clown, or the sports enthusiast, or the cheery adult friend. It's not a mixed message; it's an appropriate change, because we're no longer playing games or sitting around, hanging out, or setting the scene with an attention-grabbing activity. Now we've moved into the key teaching moment, the time for clowning, chatting or activity is passed; it's time to pay attention to what God is saying through the person who is speaking up at the front.

Remember, remember . . .

The key to all this is to keep in mind that our role is to provide training for the children and young people. Some might say we are providing reinforcement to what they are being taught at home, and that sounds excellent, ideal, thoroughly biblical and superb – and I wish the parents of the kids with whom I work were all like that! Of course they should be, but sadly they are making mistakes, or haven't really tried to instil godly attitudes into their offspring. The reality is that we can work hard every Sunday morning, and whenever else we have a chance to interact with the youngsters, but the influence of the parental style is always going to be greater.

That could, after all, be very good news. Let's hope so!

Disciplinary action

What do you do when the normal sanctions and attempts at correcting behaviour don't have the required effect? (Nice question, Elaine, and I'm glad you've asked it. It shows you've been considering these things.)

The bottom line on your Sunday morning event or youth

club or outing, or whatever the situation may be, is the enjoyment and training of as many of the participants as possible.

The goals which you have set for your meeting are not merely suggestions; they are the reason you are there. If you have no goals for your event, please ask yourself why you are staging the event at all. If it is simply because this event happens every week, then I am not so surprised that you are struggling with discipline.

You have not given up your time in order for one or two people to hijack the event and turn it into something only they have enjoyed. So you have a responsibility to the rest of the group to be the adult, to take charge and to make sure that your goals are achieved.

Obviously, the first line of action is to establish your policy. Without rules, you have nothing on which to stand, and without a disciplinary policy, you won't know what to do when the situation goes beyond the norm. Our approach is the gently-gently one.

Observe

We do not act upon reports of tale-telling by other members of the group, since they may have misinterpreted what they saw or heard, or may be bearing false witness deliberately. So we make sure that whatever rule-breaking is happening, we have seen it. There are always exceptions, of course, and the main one is where we have observed the results (damage to the fabric of the building, or injury to the body or morale of another club member).

This is followed up with a brief investigation, where possible. 'Who did this? How do you know it was them?' 'Did anyone else see?' This challenges any false witnessing, and makes sure that we are not acting upon assumptions, making dodgy accusations against the usual suspects, or anything unhelpful of that kind.

Consider the question 'Why?' in the light of Part One. Is punishment appropriate, or is sympathy? Could we have done more to provide the attention sought by the bad behaviour? Should we apologise? It's not easy!

Work as a pair

Having made the observation, or established some evidence of guilt, and having weighed up the reasons for the naughtiness, we always work as a pair to ask the accused about the incident. Asking them what happened has several advantages:

1. It's not an accusation, so there's no confrontation.
2. It shows them that our desire is to be fair.
3. It demonstrates that we do not tolerate rule-breaking.
4. It gives them a genuine chance to explain.
5. It gives them a genuine opportunity to admit fault, which is what usually happens if we've got the culprit.

Then we ask 'What do you think we should do about it?' This is not because we can't think of a punishment, but to give the guilty party a chance to consider what they have done in the context of running the group.

Love the sinner

Then we make sure that we express disapproval of the poor behaviour, but affirmation of the individual.

'You're a likeable person, but this sort of behaviour must stop, please.' The grace of God reaches even the vilest offender. Hate the sin.

Depending on the seriousness of the offence, we then explain the appropriate punishment. Usually, we issue a yellow card, warning that any further breaches of the rules of any kind will result in a ban. We have a policy to issue yellow cards (and bans) at the end of the evening, because we do not wish to exclude offenders during the course of the event, and we usually would not do this to youngsters under eleven, anyway.

Parents think they know where the youngster is, and so we have a responsibility to them to involve them if we feel the need to exclude. We will make a point of informing the young person that it is our invariable course of action to inform parents of our actions. This safeguards us from mis-understanding, since we put in writing our intentions, and it ensures that we stick to the biblical principle of letting the parents be in charge. A parent has the opportunity to challenge the punishment (none has ever done so; they almost always express gratitude to us for the efforts we have made, and show positive support toward us).

Please note that we never make threats we are not pre-pared to carry out. So we don't mention slapped legs or poisoned kittens, because we're not permitted to do these things (not that we'd want to do so, either!). But, by the same token, we don't speak darkly of banning someone unless their misbehaviour warrants this.

Temporary exclusion

If the offence warrants serious action, then we make use of the strongest possible course open to us – to exclude the young person for two weeks.

'We think you can obey the rules and have a good time here; but for the next two weeks, we ask you please not to come. Please don't turn up, because it'll be embarrassing for you when we turn you away at the door. We'll make a mark on the register so that the people on the door will know you're not allowed in next week and the week after. Once those two weeks are gone, you are very welcome to return. We would really like you to come back, and we'll forget all about it. We do expect you to obey the rules when you return, and that there will be no repeat of this offence. Is that OK? Do you understand? OK, good. Now, we will be dropping a line to your parents just to explain that you are welcome back in three weeks' time, but that you're not allowed to come next week and the week after. That's a responsibility we have to keep. All right?'

If the offence has incurred injury to someone else, we may also invite the culprit(s) to write a brief note of apology, which is simple courtesy. This request would be included in the letter to the parent also. If the offence has incurred damage to the building or the club property, we may decide to suggest to the parents that a financial contribution may be appropriate.

Now, when the disciplinary action is taking place during the Sunday morning when the parent or parents are in the building, we may even take the steps of requesting the presence of the parents. This gives us the option of excluding the youngster from the rest of our meeting, if the disruption is so severe. This places the young person in a difficult position: too naughty to stay, and not wanting to have to sit with parents in the main meeting. Hard luck, sunshine; that's what you get when you mess with me!

Your church probably has a system for calling out mothers of babies left in the crèche; use this system.

When is a short ban not enough?

Probably never. What? Yes, there are probably no disruptive children or young people who need to be given a long or a life ban. One or two youngsters have gone a few times round the cycle: two-week ban, return and reoffend, two-week ban, reoffend and so on. But very few. After a while, the parents come to one of two conclusions:

1. We cannot cope with their child, despite the evidence that we are managing well with most of the others, and have done so for years – in some cases, more years than they've been parents.
2. They are not adequately training their child.

Most realise that the chief difficulty is rooted in the way they are dealing with their child. The reasons are among those outlined in Part One.

There was one case where the parents were asked to keep their child away from the church children's events, but this was discussed at eldership level, and by mutual agreement.

CASE STUDY: MICHAEL ON THE CYCLE

An angry young man came to the youth group with a few pals, and failed every time to obey the rules. Following a few months on the ban-reoffend cycle, we had a long conversation with him.

*'Look, **Mike**, as you know, this is a Christian club. We're not embarrassed to talk about Jesus and we want you and your mates to hear what we have to say. We're interested in your opinion too, which is why we have discussions and times when you can say what you think. But we get the impression that you only come here in order to get into trouble! We've had to ask you not to come more times than we can remember. Let me make this suggestion: we're running a Christian youth group, but we don't observe even the slightest glimmer of interest coming from you. Is that right?'*

'Well, I don't believe in God and that because it's stupid.'

'Your opinion is something you're entitled to. But we are starting to wonder if this is the right time for you to come to a Christian youth club. It's clear that God's got his hands on you, and that he wants to show you that he's a loving Father. I believe the day will come when you'll recognise that. But possibly not at the moment.'

'Yeah, not at the moment. I don't believe in God.'

'I'm sorry to hear that, and I could tell you why I do believe in him. But what we're going to do is this: we've told you enough

times that you're very welcome here if you obey the rules. But you don't obey the rules, and so we have to keep on banning you. So here's what we're going to say now. We think the time for you to come to a church youth club will come along in the future. But for now, Mike, we strongly suggest that you join a secular youth club, like these two we could mention. They may well have rules that you'll find easier to keep. And then, when you've had a chance to think about it, you'll be welcome to come back here or, if time has passed and you're old enough to go to the other youth group in the church (the one for older teens), then you could give it another try. What do you think?'

'Are you chucking me out?'

'No. You are welcome here, if you obey the rules – but you haven't ever done that! We're suggesting you go elsewhere for a while and try us again. What do you think?'

'Give me those details of the other clubs.'

Evangelists who are spitting gravel at this, please note: Mike returned to the older youth club within 18 months, and was much more respectful and became a regular member. Oh yes, boisterous and outspoken; unbelieving and unrepentant. But much more likely to listen and consider the message of truth.

Summary

It is the greatest joy and privilege to be a part of the long succession of links in the chain which lead a youngster into the presence of God. It's central to the journey of faith.

People were bringing little children to Jesus to have him touch them, but the disciples rebuked them. When Jesus saw this, he was indignant. He said to them, 'Let the little children come to me, and do not hinder them, for the kingdom of God belongs to such as these. I tell you the truth, anyone who will not receive the kingdom of God like a little child will never enter it.' And he took the children in his arms, put his hands on them and blessed them. (Mark 10:13–16)

God forbid that we should establish rules and regulations which make the Christian teaching event a dry, joyless, unchildlike experience. I say let the children come in and let them be like little children, because that pleases God – and if it gets a bit noisy or chaotic, then hallelujah anyway! Let them come to Jesus and discover in him a friendly, warm, loving adult who wants the best for them, knows how to have a great laugh with them, and also shows them how to live a life to the full, in all its abundance.

Focus on the child, not the disruption. Focus on what they need, not on your preferences. Pray for them often, that they might find the joy of salvation and walk with the Lord for many years. Of course, we must keep the event safe, but please don't forget that according to Psalm 122:1, going up to the house of the Lord is supposed to be an experience full of gladness.

TO CONSIDER

1. What proportion of your team meetings is devoted to prayer?

2. Take time to set goals for each meeting, and to establish a disciplinary policy.
3. Thank God that you can be an effective link in the chain, and ask him to give you love for those in your care.

Appendix

Case Study Discussion Topics

Thanks to the marvellous and wise Linda Radcliffe for these. Chat them through at children's workers' team meetings, or with a colleague, or consider them alone. Please try to think beyond the immediate solution(s), and consider the implications of the course of action you might take, as well as trying to isolate possible causes.

1: 'We don't need you!'

For some reason, you are on your own with a group of a dozen 7–12s. One of the twelve-year-olds, who is an exceptionally bright young person, strikes up a conversation with a ten-year-old when you are trying to teach the whole group. They are giggling and talking, even though they are not usually disruptive or naughty.

2: Girls with gum

In your group of 11–14s, there are two girls who are chewing gum and talking loudly while you're speaking. You decide to move to a group activity, but these two girls refuse to take part, saying the activity is 'stupid'. One of the girls has parents in the church, but the other is from an unchurched family. What can you do?

3: Tiny Tears

One of the children in your group of 5–7s keeps crying loudly, despite your efforts to console her. She won't respond when you ask: 'What is the matter?' and the rest of the group are starting to become upset, in sympathy with her. How would you handle this situation?

4: In one ear and . . .

A six-year-old boy consistently does not do what he is told. His parents have made it clear to him that he should obey you, and have warned him that if he continues to disobey, they want to be called out of the adult meeting so that he can be disciplined. But the boy continues to be disrespectful and disobedient, so you call for the father. The father attends, takes the boy to one side and speaks firmly to him. The father returns to the adult meeting, and the boy continues to misbehave just as badly as before. What do you do now?

5: Rowdy bunch

Your group of 8–9s are involved in a group-based activity when an increasing amount of noise from the group in the next room begins to distract them. You pop your head around the door to see what all the noise is about and you notice that the leader seems to have lost control of the 6–7s. Some are wandering about, and most of them look bored. What should you do?

Children's Ministry Teaching Programme

- Do you want to see children develop a personal relationship with Jesus?

- Do you want teaching sessions that are fun, biblical, evangelical and interactive?

- Would you like children to enjoy age-appropriate activities as they learn about God?

If you've said YES to any of these questions, you need the Children's Ministry Teaching Programme.

The Children's Ministry Teaching Programme provides four leader's guides covering ages from under 3 to 13+; KidZone activity books for children aged 5-7, 7-9 and 9-11; MiniKidz and KidZone craft books for children aged 3-5 and 5-9, a magazine for those over 11; a CD of music and stories; and FamilyZone with song words, ideas for all-age worship and parents' letters.

**For more information visit our web site
www.childrensministry.co.uk**

CHILDREN'S MINISTRY

Resources

ENHANCING YOUR MINISTRY WITH CHILDREN

Reclaiming a Generation
Children – today's church, tomorrow's leaders

by Ishmael

From the author's Introduction:

'I have written this book because I believe it is time to re-evaluate our many traditions, and as we do so, I pray that it will make us more understanding of what the Bible says is expected of our children.

Before you make up your mind to agree or disagree, just look outside your window and ask yourself honestly how the thousands of lost little ones around you will ever get to know Jesus, or get to love the church, if we just stay as we are for the next two thousand years.'